GOD'S wonderful WATER

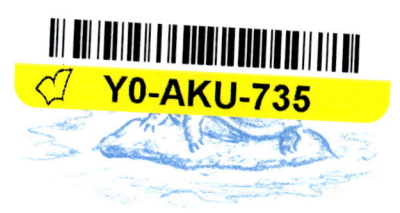

By Mary M. Landis

Artist: Virginia Kreider

Rod and Staff Publishers, Inc.
Crockett, Kentucky 41413

Code no. 90-4-97
Catalog no. 2263

Copyright 1990

By Mary M. Landis

GOD'S WONDERFUL WATER

Oceans and rivers,
Ponds and the sea,
Raindrops and snowflakes,
Falling for me.

Water is wonderful.
It is one of God's gifts to us.
Water is beautiful.
It ripples and sparkles in the sunlight.

It falls over cliffs in lovely waterfalls.

It crashes on the seashore in big waves.

Where Does Water Come From?

Water comes from springs in the ground.
Out it bubbles and flows away, making a little stream.

Water comes from wells that are deep in the earth.
We draw it from the well in buckets

Or with a hand pump

Or with an electric pump.
Out it gushes.

We drink it from a glass or cup.
"Thank You, God."

Water falls from the clouds as snowflakes.
How beautiful it is.

Water falls from the clouds as sleet and hail.
They are small pieces of ice.

Water falls from the clouds in showers.
Some showers of rain are gentle.
They make the leaves and earth all fresh and shiny.

Some rain pours from the sky with a noisy roar.
Water fills the streams and rivers, and the earth is watered.

God made water come from a rock to save the lives of many thirsty people.

Water Is the Home of Many Creatures.

It is the home of thousands of fish:
big fish and little fish, fat ones and thin ones,
all of many different shapes and colors.

Water is the home of crabs, octopuses and sharks.

Water is the home of whales, the biggest animal in the whole world.

Who Needs Water?

Trees, plants, flowers, and gardens all need water to live.

Grasshoppers, crickets, caterpillars, and spiders all need water to live.

All the animals and all the birds need water to live.

All the people and all of God's creatures need water to live.

God uses water to make rainbows.
Water is a wonderful gift from God.
"Thank You, God."